The Rastafarians

K. M. Williams

Ward Lock Educational

ISBN 0 7062 4063 4

First published 1981

Set in 11 on 12 point Times Roman
and printed by
Williamson Printing Ltd.
Davis Road, Chessington, Surrey
for Ward Lock Educational
47 Marylebone Lane
London W1M 6AX
A Pentos Company

Made in Great Britain

Contents

Acknowledgments

The author and publishers would like to thank the following for their help in supplying the photographs which illustrate this book: Johnny Allen, p. 24; Adrian Boot, pp. 41, 52, 53, 54; Camera Press, pp. 20, 26, 39, 42, 47; Ahmet Francis, pp. 19, 27, 34; James Vanderzee p. 29; Jamaican Tourist Board, p. 49; John Hillelson, p. 14; Mary Evans Picture Library, p. 8; Penguin Books Ltd., p. 6; Vernon St. Hilaire, p. 16.

We are also grateful to the following for their permission to reproduce copyright material: AFFOR for excerpts from 'Talking Blues'; Bogle-L'Ouverture Publications for excerpts from *Dread, Beat and Blood* and an excerpt from *Down De Road* by Linton Kwesi Johnson; Heinemann Educational Books for an excerpt from *The Rastafarians* by Leonard E. Barrett; Oxford University Press for an excerpt from 'Wings of a Dove' from *Rights of Passage* by Edward Brathwaite.

Note
This book is the result of several years of insistence from my students that Rastafarianism should be studied in school. They feel that it is crucial that black faiths take their place in a multi-faith society. Besides this, the Rastafarians are so *visible* and intriguing, and so misunderstood.

However, this book would not have been produced without the help of Frankie Leibe.

K.M.W.

Introduction

Red, yellow, black and green woollen hats, worn by young black men, weaving their way through the crowded streets of London, Birmingham or other big cities, are an eye-catching sight, as is the sound of the reggae music which is so much associated with them. Other groups of young people indicate their loyalties, maybe with football scarves, badges, denims, or fashionable gear, but the hats and favours of the Rastafarians are quite different, for the colours are the symbols of their religion. The meaning of these colours is part of a story which started in the horrifying days of the Atlantic Slave Trade, and develops in an exciting, fearful and courageous way in the poor areas of urban Jamaica, and which is currently being told wherever young black people feel the need to stress their identity.

Not all the people who wear the colours *are* Rastafarians, and there are others who are passionate believers, who wear neither the dreadlocks, the long plaited hair, or any mark of their loyalty. Many in the black community are very unsympathetic to the cause. Many in the white community remain quite ignorant of what it all means. And, because they dress and behave in such a special and different way, the Rastafarians are easy to pick out for blame, when there is tension or crime.

The Rastafarians gives you the chance to understand this new and original religion. It is Bible-based, but not Christian. And this book looks at the roots of that faith, its language and what it means, and its music which has become part of a world-wide cult. Many of its ideas will seem strange at first, but you will begin to see that its members have made a relevant, clear faith from their history, their lives, and their suffering.

And since it is a 'young' religion in every sense you will be able to watch it develop and change, to be an observer of one of the most exciting religious movements today. In fact, you may be able to write the next chapter in the story of the Rastafarians.

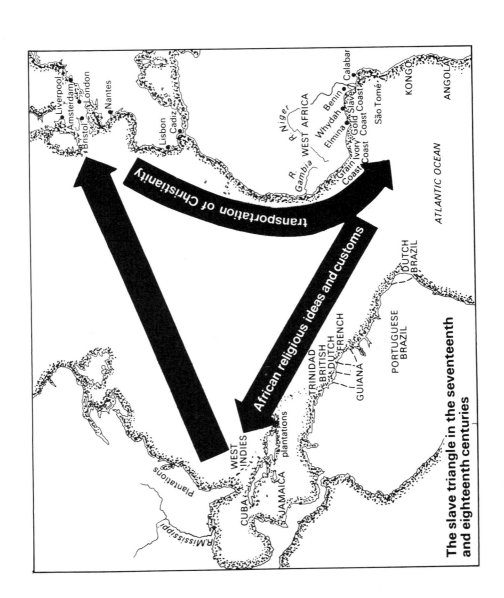

The slave triangle in the seventeenth and eighteenth centuries

Liverpool
Amsterdam
Bristol London
Nantes
Lisbon
Cadiz

R. Niger
WEST AFRICA
R. Gambia
Benin Calabar
Whydah
Elmina Gold Slave
Ivory Coast Coast
Grain Coast
São Tomé
KONGO
ANGOLA

ATLANTIC OCEAN

transportation of Christianity

African religious ideas and customs

R. Mississippi
plantations
CUBA
JAMAICA
WEST INDIES
plantations
TRINIDAD
BRITISH
DUTCH
FRENCH
GUIANA
DUTCH BRAZIL
PORTUGUESE BRAZIL

1 The setting in Jamaica

The early days

As early as 1509 Spaniards had brought slaves to Jamaica. Although they were Roman Catholic in name, the slaves had continued to worship their own God. By 1655 the British had driven out the Spaniards and the native Arawaks were extinct. Now the Anglican Church was recognized as the official Church, but it was not considered necessary, sensible or safe, to teach slaves about Christianity. It was argued that it was far too complex for them to understand. On the other hand, should the slaves discover too much, they might be fired by the revolutionary nature of the Christian message. The plantation owners did not consider that the doctrines of salvation, equality and brotherly love applied to their slaves.

Great care had been taken in not allowing slaves from similar places to settle together in Jamaica. This was to prevent their co-operating in rebelling against their owners. Nevertheless they had shared similar enough religious practices and beliefs in West Africa for them to retain and continue them as much as possible in slavery. In addition, some of their own religious leaders had been enslaved, and they helped to keep African beliefs alive.

Street preacher

Celebration at Emancipation

All black people had brought with them a tradition of singing, dancing and drumming which had been used in religious communications, to praise, to exhort and to enact myth and legend. From most groups came a knowledge of ecstatic religious behaviour, when gods operated in or through men who might be 'possessed', or might be prophets.

When Emancipation came in 1835, Christianity spread fast. Swiftly black Churches began to break away. These Churches often included African beliefs and ways of worship.

In 1929 the American Pentecostalists arrived. Both the Pentecostal and Revival Churches stressed the power of healing and had inspiring leaders who attracted large followings. They also allowed African elements in worship. The members of these Churches were mainly the poor black people who formed the majority of the population.

Emancipation

The Abolition of Slavery in Jamaica in 1835 did not 'free' the black people in any sense except the legal one. In order to live they had to farm and fish as well as work on the plantations.

When blacks tried to improve their lot by leaving the rural areas and moving, to Kingston in particular, their chance of finding work was poor, and living conditions were completely inadequate. In the first half of this century, with a quarter of the island's population, Kingston had slums as desperate as any in the world, where the poorest literally scavenged off the 'dungle', the refuse of the better-off, in order to survive.

For some, the churches provided comfort. Others looked outside the island for an alternative solution. Since slaves had been brought unwillingly to the West Indies, now that they had been freed, some men dreamed of returning to Africa. These men, prophets in their time, looked 'Back to Africa', to Ethiopia in particular. This drive back to Africa is called Ethiopianism since, for them, Africa and Ethiopia are interchangeable terms. Ethiopianism, particularly as set out by Marcus Garvey (see p. 28), although not a religion, was a direct forerunner and stimulus to Rastafarianism.

For Garveyites and other Ethiopianists, the coronation of Ras Tafari (Prince of the House of Tafari), the warlord great-grandson of King Sahaka Selassie of Shoa in 1930, fulfilled the prophecy of Psalm 68,'Princes shall come out of Ethiopia, and Ethiopia shall stretch forth her hands unto God.'

Four acquaintances: Joseph Hibbert (page 31), Leonard Howell (page 31), Archibald Dunkley and Robert Hinds had independent revelations that Haile Selassie was the Messiah of the Black People, and together with Paul Earlington, Vernal Davis and Ferdinand Ricketts they founded the Ras Tafari faith — choosing Haile Selassie's name, rather than his titles. The religion is now generally referred to by outsiders as 'Rastafarianism', and its adherents as Rastafarians, Rastamen or Rastas. Members may give themselves titles, such as 'Prince'; others refer to themselves as 'Brother'.

What to accept, what to reject?
In creating their own religious faith, Rastafarians have accepted, rejected and reordered elements from existing Churches.

African religious beliefs and practices are rejected as false and superstitious. Sorcerers (*obeah* men and women in Jamaica) are dangerous. They waste energy and distract the black man from his religious duties. *Myal,* or possession by spirits, the other major African manifestation, can only be repugnant to a Rasta, who aspires to *discover*, not *possess,* his divinity which already lies within him. Rastas are bitterly opposed to 'white' churches, and Pentecostalism is rejected as a diseased version of a white Church. For the black man all other religions except Rastafarianism are false because they cripple him spiritually and degrade him socially.

Rastafarians consider the Bible 'inerrant' or incapable of untruth. Above all, Rastafarianism stresses an interpretation of the Bible which emphasizes life and love for the true follower, and does not dwell on sin and punishment or death.

What has been taken from existing religions, is the use of parts of the Bible, the role of prophets, and many of the African elements in styles of worship.

Many established churches in Jamaica echo the British style and the buildings and institutions of these denominations are rejected by Rastafarians who generally worship in the open air

The Ethiopian Orthodox Church

The sole Church to receive recognition by Rastafarians, (but only in a guarded way), is the Ethiopian Orthodox Church, a branch of which was established in Jamaica in 1969, and which has about 7,000 members, some of whom are Rastas. As a whole the movement has very mixed feelings about the Church, since they consider it surprisingly 'Christian'. There are good reasons, nevertheless, why many Rastas go there.

It is not a 'Western' Church. It came at the express invitation of the Jamaican Government, and largely on Rasta initiative. Its foundation is shrouded in mystery. It separated from the Western Church and the Eastern Orthodox Church over the question of Jesus Christ, whom the followers believe has only a divine nature. They do not believe in Original Sin, or Purgatory. Eucharist is accompanied by cymbals, bells, drums, rattles, singing and dancing, and richly-adorned vestments contribute to visually beautiful services. At the head of the Church is the Abuna. Until he died, this was Haile Selassie, living God of the Rastafarians. Rastafarians baptized into the Church retained their locks and beards, but argued against being baptized in the home of Jesus Christ rather than Haile Selassie.

2 Rastafarian beliefs, myths and symbols

The central beliefs

Rastafarianism is a Biblical religion. The Bible is used as a source of inspiration, interpretation and information. There is always room for disagreement about the information, because the individual is left great freedom in interpretation, innovation and improvisation. Much Rastafarian thought evolves from continuing debates or 'reasoning'.

Another result of members' freedom in interpretation is that the initial beliefs have been considerably adapted as social and religious situations have altered. In 1953 there were six central ideas:

1 Black men are reincarnations of the ancient Israelites and were exiled to the West Indies because of their transgressions.
2 Haile Selassie is the living God and Emperor of the World.
3 Ethiopia is heaven. The Jamaican situation is hopeless hell.
4 Black men are superior to white men. They will soon rule the world.
5 Soon black men will avenge themselves on white men.
6 Their God and Emperor will soon arrange for them to return to their homeland, Ethiopia.

By 1960 these had been reduced to four:

1 Ras Tafari is the living God.
2 Ethiopia is the black man's home.
3 Repatriation is the way of redemption for the black man. It will occur shortly.
4 The ways of the white man are evil, particularly for the black man.

A year later the beliefs had been refined further:

1 Ras Tafari is the true and living God.
2 Salvation for the black man can only come through repatriation to Africa, i.e. Ethiopia.

In 1981 it is probable that while all Rastafarians would agree with the first belief, only half would believe in repatriation to Africa; but, for most, 'redemption by repatriation' continues to be desirable, even if the journey is spiritual rather than earthly.

The Bible

The Bible was generally the only book available to the ex-slaves, who treated it with great respect. They found in it fabulous stories of the Continent from which they had been taken, stories which countered their humiliation and degradation.

Rastafarians believe that Egypt and Ethiopia were both in Africa (*Psalm* 68:12), and Ethopia and Africa came to mean the same thing. It followed that the Hamites and Cushites who inhabited this country were black and out of this country would come a Messiah: 'And I saw a strong angel proclaiming . . . behold the Lion of the Tribe of Judah, the root of David' (*Revelations* 5:2); 'The King of Kings' (*Revelations* 19:16).

Although black men had been taken away from Africa, when this divine King was crowned, all his sons would be free to return to Him. He had revealed himself three times already in Moses, Elijah and Jesus Christ, and when He came finally, all the black man's anguish would be finished.

Ras Sam Brown, (see page 33), says that these beliefs are not handed down from son to son, as in Christianity. Each man discovers them for himself. Then his duty is not only to free himself and all oppressed Ethiopians (scattered black people) but to liberate all persecuted people, animals, herbs and all life forms.

Interpretation of the Bible

Rastafarian interpretation of the Bible is selective. This is because, despite its sacred quality, Rastafarians must always be guarded and painstaking in their study of it, because they are very suspicious. They realize that their version of the Bible is that of a white man, King James. Some brothers believe that it is a collection of Rastafarian lore, and that Jewish appropriation of it is false, since Rastafarians are the true (black) Israelites. Others deny that it is a translation. Many of the books, especially of the New Testament, are omitted from close study, as being irrelevant.

The Rastafarian starts from certain theories, and his study of the Bible supports them. The theories are tested and proved correct.

Son-ship to God

The Bible proves the Rastafarian's son-ship to God, Haile Selassie, and the individual carries this divinity within himself; hence the significance of the term 'I and I'. Because God inhabits each man, his body becomes a temple and therefore there is no need for churches or formal workship.

'Peace and love'

God is love, and love is pre-eminent. It created the world. Evil is the work of Beelzebub, but the Bible says that he has been destroyed already. A Rastafarian achieves a state of respect for himself and love for others through the use of cannabis and a peaceful lifestyle, hence his greeting 'Peace and love!'

Myths and symbols

Africa

Africa is the object of devotion as the home of Haile Selassie, and a territory for which the Rastafarian longs, as his Motherland. God created Africa from 'the stone hewed out of the mountain without hands' (*Daniel* 2:31). Very few Rastafarians have visited Africa, and therefore general knowledge about it is based on Biblical study, together with readings of articles about Ethiopia, such as those produced by the *National Geographic Magazine* at the time of Haile Selassie's coronation.

The ancient source of the black man's history is seen originally in the scattering of the twelve tribes of Israel. The spirit of the Lord went into Ethiopia. There the Queen of Sheba came to Solomon, ruler of the black tribe, and learned all his wisdom. Because they then learned God's true Way, they became the Chosen People.

Haile Selassie, Ras Tafari

Because he is a twentieth-century figure, it is possible to look at both the man and the myth, Ras Tafari (Prince of the House of Tafari)

Haile Selassie

14

who chose the title Haile Selassie, Might of the Trinity, thus fulfilling the prophecy of *Revelations* 5 and 19. The recognition of the divinity of Haile Selassie is foretold in *Psalm* 68. 'Princes shall come out of Egypt; Ethiopia shall soon stretch forth her hands unto God.'

In Jamaican eyes part of the power of his coronation in 1930 lay in the attention the whole world directed on Ethiopia. It was as if everyone acknowledged Haile Selassie's kingship, including the white kings and queens of Europe. When Italy invaded Ethiopia in 1935, the prophecy was fulfilled.

Great power is invested in his titles:
Haile Selassie,
King of Kings,
Lion of Judah,
Negus of Ethiopia.

The Lion

Rastafarians believe that Haile Selassie, Lion of Judah, united in his power the human and animal world. It is said that he was fearless. Lions roamed in his garden, and slept at his feet. The royal animal, particuarly the head and mane, occurs frequently in Rastafarian paintings, and as an image in poetry. The mane inspires some of the most elaborate teasing out and extraordinary shapes of the dreadlocks' hair. The proud, dignified walk of the lion is consciously copied by Rastafarians, for however inferior other Jamaicans may think them, Rastafarians contradict this belief in their regal bearing.

The dreadlocks

It is said that in the early days of the movement in Jamaica the Rastafarians adopted uncut hair because it was impossible to look after their hair 'in the wilderness'. The effect that the uncut hair and beard created was awesome, dreadful and hence the term 'dreadlock'. The locks help brethren to identify with the warriors of the Old Testament, and the Masai and Galla tribesmen of Africa; in addition they recall the power of Samson's hair and his destructions of thousands of Philistines.

A dread flashes his locks, harnessing power, creating awe

In worship, while women keep their heads covered, men expose and 'flash' their locks, as if they were conducting lightning.

Red, black, green, gold
If you have seen a group of Rastafarians in Britain you will have seen them wearing these colours - maybe in the knitted tam they wear covering their locks. The colours have great significance:
Red represents the blood of the martyrs, the slaves and the brethren.
Black represents the skin; it is synonymous with holiness, fire and creativity.
Green is for Ethiopia, and for the ganja herb, and Jamaica.
Gold is for the Rastafarian faith and for Jamaica.

Old Testament themes
The scattering
This was initially of the tribes of Israel. Slavery further dispersed black people throughout the world. The final scattering was when workers migrated after the Second World War.

16

Punishment

This is the time spent out of Africa, oppressed by the white man. It is the loss of identity through slavery, and the humiliation caused by white governments.

The exile and return

The place of exile is Babylon. Babylon is seductive and destructive, pitiless and corrupt. Exile is spent under the rule of Rome, because Rome is the originator of false white Christian Churches and the oppression which they brought. The black man can be seduced by Christianity. It is in the nature of his 'repatriation' that he will have to discover the heresy of Christianity.

In the 1950s it was thought that repatriation, the return from exile, might be achieved by immigration into the United Kingdom, but that hope proved an illusion, and for Rastafarian immigrants, Britain became Babylon. So, too, did the United States and Canada where Jamaicans migrated after their entry to Britain was limited.

Rastafarian lore has it that the black peoples of the world should have been able to return to Africa at Emancipation had they not been cheated: £2,000,000 had been sent to Jamaica by Queen Victoria for this purpose, but the slave-owners diverted it into their own pockets.

Some twenty Rastafarians have settled about two hundred miles from Addis Ababa through a scheme administered by the Ethiopian World Federation.

An essential part of the Rastafarian identity is to be an alien and an outcast. Waiting for the return *is* being a Rastafarian. So is the sense of imminent departure. As social situations alter, the territory of Zion, the place of hope, is always one country ahead.

Time

The ancient narrative of Rastafarian history is 'fabulous'. While the past and future are glorious, the present is used in preparation for the imminent departure through prayer and scholarship. Time is created, not wasted, when used peacefully and passively. There is no interest in conventional dates or chronology.

Reincarnation

This is a very important belief, important in itself and also because it relates to Rastafarian rejection of death. Most members are quite young, so they do not encounter death very frequently, but reincarnation helps them to deny it when it does occur. Some do not accept the fact of Haile Selassie's death (see page 54).

3   Rituals and the Rastafarian lifestyle

The simplest things may have many meanings. The greeting 'Peace and Love!' is also a prayer and statement of faith. The main Rastafarian rituals are concerned with daily behaviour, collective workship and the use of ganja.

Prayer and daily observances
In their lives Rastafarians attempt to act out their religious beliefs. They pray daily: 'So we hail our God, Selassie-I, Eternal God, Ras Tafari, hear us and help us, and cause Thy face to shine upon us, Thy children.'

Although the title 'Ras Tafari' is the name chosen for the faith, Haile Selassie is also used in prayers and songs. 'Jah' is a powerful term probably contracted from Jehovah, and can be added as in 'Jah-Ras-Tafari'.

Meetings
These need not be held at weekly intervals. They may be very small, with a few brethren visiting the yard of a leader, or very large, as when thousands converge on a camp. At meetings prophets interpret God's message as conveyed through their visions. They inspire and enthuse members. The activities of the meetings will include prayers, chanting, singing, drumming and preaching. In preparation for a meeting, members will have adhered 'very strictly' to food and moral taboos and may well have fasted in order to purify themselves and heighten their awareness. Although not compulsory except at a Nyabingi, most people will smoke ganja in a ritual way; a term used to describe this is 'taking the chalice'.

Between 1890 and 1920 in East Africa, there was a cult of protest called Nyabingi. It is rumoured that Haile Selassie led it, and it has given its name to the great ceremonial meetings of the cult. Whereas an outsider might be tolerated at an ordinary meeting, he would be unwise to try to attend a Nyabingi. The mood of these meetings is intense, ecstatic and overwhelming.

Three large drums beat double membranes of goat skin stretched over rum kegs. The 'voice', the repeater drum, gives the melody, to which the funde adds syncopation, and the big bass drum gives the rhythm. One theme can be sustained for an hour.

Young Rastafarians gather to 'reason' with an Elder at a Meeting in the country

The dialogue between 'voice' and 'chorus' is emphasized in the ritual chanting which builds up, and then sustains, the religious fervour. Christian hymns and tunes are adapted, and new lyrics created by prophets and poets.

Voice	How did we get here?
Chorus	Slavery!
Voice	Who brought us here?
Chorus	The white man!
	He tells us we are inferior
	But we know that we are not!
	We are superior!
Voice	Ethiopia?
Chorus	Yes!
Voice	England?
Chorus	No!
	Let my people go!

The emotional impact of a large meeting is overwhelming. They are usually held at camps far out in the hills. Two thousand

Three Rastas wearing the typical dreadlocks gather with a 'nubbie', a younger follower, to smoke the Holy Herb

members may gather, with the symbolic colours in their clothes and decorating their prayer staves. The scene is illuminated by leaping fires and flaming torches, and the brethren gradually reach a state of ecstasy, stimulated by the communal experience and expectation, the power of the ganja, and the deafening accompaniment of drums, chanting and hymns over a powerful sound system.

Ganja
The use of ganja (cannabis) probably began in the early days of the movement, out in the wilderness retreat of the hills, where it was possible to cultivate it successfully. By no means all members use ganja. Some use it for medicinal purposes only as a herbal remedy and infuse it as a tea, but its use at meetings always follows the same pattern, and it is treated as a sacrament, reverently.

It dispels gloom and fear, induces visions, and heightens the feelings, creating a sensation of fellow love and peace. Although its use is associated in the public's eyes with crime, it has not proved possible to connect the use of ganja by true Rastafarians with crime.

Ganja is known as the Wisdom Weed, the Holy Herb. Members who live in the hills grow it in gardens, where it flourishes. They argue that they produce only that ganja needed for Rastafarian rituals, and to get involved in the larger drug traffic would be to abuse its sacred quality.

Its use was probably introduced by Asian indentured labourers in the nineteenth century, but is said by some to have been a gift from the Arawaks, the original inhabitants, or to have been a divine gift, or to have been inherited from the first enslaved Africans, who brought it with them.

The ganja experience
In describing his experiences, the Rastafarian is ultra-sensitive. He may be passive, but he suffers — and he takes on the suffering of his history and all oppressed blacks. He still feels the slave driver's whip in Babylon, as Marley (see p. 51) sings in *Slave Driver:*

Every time I hear a crack of the whip,
My blood runs cold
I remember the slave ship
How they brutalize my very soul.

The Rastafarian would call this point of total commitment/ identification/revelation 'headrest', or 'indwell' with Jah. The brother endeavours to journey through the everyday world as if it really is the territory of black experience. The poet Edward Brathwaite describes how the pilgrim progresses to Zion in Kingston, or London, or Birmingham, or New York:

And I
Rastafar-I
In Babylon's boom
town, crazed by the moon
and the peace of this chalice, I
prophet and singer, scourge
of the gutter, guardian
Trench Town, the Dungle and Young's
Town, rise and walk through the now silent
streets of affliction, hawk's eyes
hard with fear, with
affection, and hear my people
cry, my people
shout:

The use of ganja is paradoxical, for although its use generates peace and love, it is illegal, and brings the members into conflict with the law, emphasizing the fact that they are outsiders. For the majority of people, making war on the Rastas and on ganja is the same thing. There is an added problem in punishing the ganja user, too, in that if he is a 'religious' user, the punishment may make him a martyr in the eyes of others, and martyrs feed the faith.

The religious life of a Rastafarian
The visions of the prophets and the individual revelations of the member are vivid climaxes in the religious life of the Rastafarian. He looks both inward to his own divinity, and to other members for confirmation of their brotherly love. The public may deride and despise him, but that rejection only makes his faith more solid. His conviction that it is *he* who is the Chosen, becomes firmer. Middle class Jamaicans may say that the Rastafarian is lazy and lawless, pretending a religion to hide his dislike of work but all this proves to the Rastafarian is that the socially privileged have not so far 'come into consciousness'. All men are potentially Rastafarians in that 'the doctrine is in them at birth', and the point at which a man recognizes that is like a spiritual conversion.

Language
One way in which the Rastafarian separates himself from other men is through his language. It takes elements from available languages, particularly Jamaican Creole, ghetto dialects, Old Testament English, Standard English and the language of hallucination. It is not easily understood by an outsider: if spoken by an illiterate man it may sound incoherent, if by an articulate one it becomes 'word magic'. It expresses the expanding self-awareness of the Rastafarian, and describes his visions, as well as the needs of his everyday life.

Breaking the code
Much of the meaning of Rastafarian dialogue remains hidden in the shared experiences of the speakers — in the past as slaves, and in the present self-perception as dispossessed and rejected. The speaker asserts his independence as a *person* not a *thing*. Therefore the language becomes intensely personal — in grammatical terms, the 'object case' is practically omitted. Verbs are simplified or left out. This makes the language very passive. Prepostions are limited, so relationship between people and things are made denser.

The emphasis is on 'I', the singular/plural 'I and I' also conveying man's double nature. 'I' may also replace part of a name or a word as in:

Haile Selassie-I
I - vine - Divine
I - thiopian - Ethiopian.

If you look at lyrics by Rastafarian groups, you will see how intense and compacted the style can be.

In addition to these significant grammatical features, the Rastafarian uses certain devices in his speech including proverbs, riddles, paradoxes and parables. In fact these are naturally assimilated from the oral tradition of the island, but an outsider needs a detailed knowledge of the references to untangle the 'real' meanings. Proverbs transmit concentrated wisdom; riddles tease with their contradicting statements; in paradox — as in riddles — apparently opposite elements meet and interact; in parable one meaning may be drawn by analogy from another.

All these characteristics enable the member to explain himself, in religious and social terms.

The moral life

The method of achieving ecstacy is self-discipline. A man goes down deep inside himself; then he must search intensely. Receptive and passive, he must then wait until he is aware of a call which will direct him and instruct him.

The laws by which a Rastafarian conducts his social and moral life are strict and give him a perspective from which to judge his personal discoveries. The code is firm, and very close to that laid down by the Old Testament. In a society where behaviour is motivated by its desire to acquire possessions, Rastafarian lifestyle is ascetic, self-denying.

Ras Sam Brown (see page 33) formulated this version of the code.

1 We strongly object to sharp implements, used in the desecration of the figure of Man, e.g. trimming and shaving, tattooing of the skin, and cutting of the flesh.
2 We are basically vegetarians making scant use of certain flesh, outlawing the use of swine's flesh in any form, shell fishes, scaleless fishes (predators), snails etc.
3 We worship and observe no other God but Rastafari, outlawing all other forms of pagan worship, yet respecting all believers.
4 We love and respect the brotherhood of mankind, yet our first love is to the sons of Ham (i.e. black men).

5   We disapprove and abhor utterly, hate, jealousy, envy, deceit, guile, treachery etc.
6   We do not agree to the pleasures of present-day society and its modern evils.
7   We are avowed to create a world of one brotherhood.
8   Our duty is to extend the hand of charity to any brother in distress firstly, for he is of the Rastafari Order — secondly, to any human, animal, plants etc.
9   We do adhere to the ancient laws of Ethiopia (i.e. Old Testament Law).
10 Thou shalt give no thought to the aid, titles and possessions that the enemy in his fear may seek to bestow on you; resolution to your purpose is the love of Rastafari.

This code has been elaborated. Food taboos are very strict. In addition to the general prohibitions, no salt or processed food is allowed. No rum, milk or coffee may be drunk, only fruit juices. Tobacco is forbidden. All food is very carefully grown, and prepared

A Rastafarian family in their London home

24

with scrupulous cleanliness. Rastafarian food is pure and 'I-tal'. No menstruating woman is allowed to prepare food for her man.

The role of women

Rastafarianism is a male-orientated and male dominated religion. Negative associations and myths are invariably embodied in stories about the seductive nature of women. The role of the woman is that of an individual queen to her partner. Fidelity is expected of her, and any sexual misdemeanours forbidden by the Old Testament, which is also used to prove the acceptability of male infidelity. Birth control is rejected as a white ploy to murder black people, contravening the Old Testament prophecy that 'the seeds of Israel shall be numberless.' During menstruation a woman is considered unclean.

Rasta women dress with modesty and every daughter and sister develops her own sense of propriety. They are rarely seen without their heads wraps of colourful printed cotton and their dress lengths vary from midcalf to the floor. Rastafarian women move with a serene sense of dignity, with a natural and balanced awareness of themselves and their own beauty and grace. 'A woman is what she is or isn't born with and her worth in life is relative only to her acceptance of Rastfari, the resultant peace and love within herself and her contribution to her family and community. *(Nichols)*

Owning to high unemployment, and their principles, many Rastafarians are unable or unwilling to work so the responsibility of earning the money to support her man and her children falls to the woman. In effect, despite their convictions, the men may be dependent on their women. In this sense, the lot of the Rastafarian woman is not dissimilar to that of the Jamaican woman in general as Louise Bennett explains in her *Jamaica 'Oman.*

Jamaica 'Oman
is how dem ginal soh!
Look how long dem liberated
An de man dem never know!

Neck an neck an foot an foot wid man
She buckle hole her own,
Wile man a call her 'so-so rib'
'Oman a tun backbone.

God made men and women to serve; man in his way, woman in hers.

A typical yard. In these close communities Rastafarian ideas were first developed and spread quickly

Rastafarian life and the larger community

Rastafarians prefer to live in 'yards' or communities separate from other groups. This may be forced upon them by poverty, anyway, if they live in shanty towns or in rural areas. Despite their poverty, their

One form of Rastafarian art is mask making. The mask both celebrate the religion and echo African masks.

strict moral code allows them to live in a relatively dignified way, as long as they have access to subsistence farming or fishing, and ganja.

Those men who do get jobs object to paying taxes to the Jamaican administration saying that their loyalty is to Haile Selassie, and when they appear in court, which is not infrequently, they affirm, refusing to swear on the Bible.

They dislike sending their children to school, considering that much of what they are taught is untrue, immoral and indoctrination. Ironically, the Haile Selassie Junior School refuses to accept children with locks.

The ganja-smoking, dreadlock-wearing Rastafarian is at the militant, expressive end of the religious spectrum. There is no obligation to smoke ganja continually or to wear dreadlocks. However, the locksman will not use a comb, although his hair needs careful tending and teasing into shape. When Rastafarians depend on the larger community, they may moderate their style those with cut hair are the 'Afro-combsome', unbearded Rastafarians are 'Cleanface', and adolescents without beard growth are 'Nubbies'.

4 The prophets

Christian scholars explain their views and opinions by writing about them. Rastafarians explain their views and opinions by talking about them. Their beliefs are proved by reading and reinterpreting the Old Testament. Each man can be his own theologian. In practice, ideas and interpretations are presented by prophet leaders, whose revelations are so inspired that they draw followers to them. These men are like spiritual adventurers and their visions are extraordinary. The prophet must interpret his ecstasies so that his followers increase in faith and enthusiasm.

Marcus Garvey
The most powerful prophet of Ethiopianism was Marcus Garvey, created first National Hero of Independent Jamaica. He is also regarded by Rastafarians as their greatest contemporary prophet.

Born in 1867 in St Ann's Bay, Jamaica, he died in London in 1940. During his life he travelled widely, and worked for his cause with great industry. Ironically he died without having visited Africa.

Marcus Mosiah Garvey was one of only two surviving children from a family of eleven. His family were quite well off and it was only when his friendship with a white girl was severed when they were fourteen, that he began to realize the implications of being black. Apprenticed to his godfather, a printer, he revelled in life in Kingston, and in reading in the family's library.

From an early age, he involved himself in Union affairs on the side of those less fortunate than himself. Unable to get a secure job because of his reputation as black leader and troublemaker, in 1910 he started the first of a series of newspapers to put across his views to as wide an audience as possible. *Garvey's Watchtower* was not successful, so he set off for the island of Costa Rica, where he recognized the oppression of the black plantation workers and published *La Nacionale*. In Panama it was the working conditions of the black labourers on the Canal that disturbed him and *La Prensa* was published. Learning all the time about the oppression of the black people, he travelled to the United States, via Eduador, Nicaragua, Honduras, Colombia and Venuzuela. Any attempts to further his cause in informing the people of their common predicament were frustrated when he returned to Jamaica, so he left for London, where he was able to learn much more about Africa, which from now on was to give his endeavours a focus and a direction.

Back in Jamaica in 1914 with five friends, he founded *The United Negro Improvement Society (UNIA)*, 'uniting all the Negro People of the World' with its call 'One God! One Aim! One Destiny!' Their aim was, he said 'to lay down our burdens, and rest our weary backs and feet by the banks of the Niger, and sing our songs, and chant our hymns to the God of Ethiopia.'

In 1918 he founded a journal called *The Negro World,* which reached a circulation of 200,000.

In 1920 he organized the *First International Convention of Negro Peoples of the World* in New York. There 25,000 delegates represented 25 countries, coming together to formulate a Declaration of Rights for Negro People. Garvey was elected Provisional President of Africa and it was decided that there should be a symbolic Black House in Washington.

In order to develop commerce, and communication, and merchant-navy capacity to help repatriate Negroes to Africa, the Black Star Line was founded, and in the United States, factories, cooperatives, stores, restaurants and publishing houses were set up, together with organizations under the wing of the Association, which would organize themselves in disciplined and military-like groups.

Marcus Garvey

In this way pride and solidarity were engendered. Negroes, Garvey said, 'had a beautiful history, and shall create another'. Repatriation to Africa was to be the central aim. 'Let Africa be our guiding Star,' he said, 'our Star of Destiny.' With the voice of a prophet, he encouraged Negroes to prepare, for 'No-one knows when the hour of Africa's Redemption cometh. It is in the wind. It is coming. One day, like a storm, it will come.'

To the principle of repatriation was added the duty to liberate the oppressed peoples in Africa.

In 1921 Garvey founded the African Orthodox Church in New York, and its first bishop was consecrated through the Greek Orthodox Church. Garvey's statements about the religion and its associations with Ethiopia were ambiguous: 'We Negroes believe in the God of Ethiopia, the everlasting God . . . We shall worship Him though the spectacles of Ethiopia . . .' However it was not long before Bishop George McGuire was preaching that God Himself was black; it followed that the Madonna and Christ were black too.

As a result of mismanagement of the Black Star Shipping Line Garvey went to prison in the United States. While he was in prison he is reported to have spoken in prophetic tones, and in language which seized the imagination of the early Rastafarians.

> When I am dead, wrap the mantle of red, black and green around me. For in the new life, I will rise with God's grace and blessing to lead the millions up the heights of triumph with the colours that you'll know. Look for me in the whirlwind or the storm, look for me all around you, for with God's grace, I shall come and bring with me countless black slaves who have died in America and in the West Indies and the millions in Africa to aid you in the fight for liberty, freedom and life.

The flag of the *UNIA* was made of red, for the blood of martyrs, black for the skin of the Negro, and green for the lush vegetation of Africa, the Motherland. Rastafarians incorporated those colours within their symbolism, as they did Garvey's promise of a Second Coming in their belief in reincarnation. He spoke, too, of redemption of black peoples and their eventual unity. His vision was incorporated into 'A Petition of the Negro Races' which he presented to the League of Nations in 1928.

The early prophets
While Marcus Garvey was in America, his followers were very disorganized in Jamaica, and instead of uniting their efforts, they split into several different movements and followed various leaders.

Between the two World Wars, there was considerable tension on the island, and this showed itself in various ways. The Nyabingi Cult of East Africa not only contributed its name to the large ceremonial meetings of the Rastafarians, but individuals who sympathized with the cult's aims modelled themselves along its anti-white lines. Some of them were later incorporated in the more violent fringes of Rastafarianism.

A more modest following built up round Alexander Bedward of August Town. However there was considerable excitement when he announced that he would achieve his own ascension by rising to heaven, on December 11 1920. A large crowd gathered at Mona near Kingston — and on the subsequent days when the elevation failed to materialize. He was removed to a hospital.

It was not until Haile Selassie's coronation in 1930, that there was a revival of zeal, and it appeared that Garvey's prophecies were to be fulfilled.

Joseph Hibbert

Joseph Hibbert was born in 1894 and lived for twenty years in Costa Rica. He had been a Freemason, a member of the Ancient Order of Ethiopia. Immediately after the Coronation of Haile Selassie he returned to Jamaica and founded the Ethiopian Mystic Masons. He was a strong leader who founded many new Rastafarian groups.

Leonard Howell

Leonard Howell was slightly older than Hibbert, and had fought in the Ashanti Wars in 1896 in the Gold Coast (Ghana). He is one of the few brethren to have a personal knowledge of Africa, shown in the several African languages which he learned to speak. He had visited the United States and returned to Jamaica in 1930. In 1934 he founded the Ethiopian Salvation Society. However he was arrested almost immediately afterwards in St Thomas, while preaching. The authorities thought he was encouraging people to rebel against the Government. He advocated the six principles which became the founding principles of the faith and which remained relatively unaltered until the 1950s (see page 12).

Harrassed in the towns, he retreated into the hills of St Catherine and lived rather like a chief. The commune, called Pinnacle, had between 500 to 1,500 members at its most powerful. It was said that he took thirteen wives, and grew and smoked cannabis. It seems certain that he tried to force his neighbours to pay taxes to him, as Haile Selassie's regent, but this coercion failed because they told the police.

Life at Pinnacle from the early days was tightly disciplined. The day was split into two activities: agriculture and education. Commune members learned African history and Amharic, the language of Ethiopia. The Bible, particularly the Old Testament, was studied rigorously.

Howell's reputation was enhanced when he 'miraculously' evaded police during a raid in 1941, though he was later prosecuted, found guilty, and imprisoned. He used his time in prison for contemplation and by the end of two years he had considerably elaborated early Rastafarian thinking, and supplemented the central doctrines.

Hair was to be grown into locks, so deliberately inviting scorn and stigma. The Divinity was redefined, and in an extraordinary act of faith the distance between man and God shrank until it could be encompassed in 'I and I'. Howell's persecution produced converts for the faith and encouraged other men to have visions and become prophets, and, as could have been expected, they were despised, rejected and spurned.

A decade later Pinnacle was reestablished. There was increased conflict with the police, and in 1954 the commune was dispersed, most of its members finding protection in the slum area of Kingston called Back O' Wall.

The cult's ideas spread more rapidly than ever in the densely-populated slums. The group reestablished itself yet again, though only briefly, because Howell finally moved from interpreting God's visions, to identifying himself with God, and was committed to hospital.

Martimmo Planno

A prophet who has been influential for twenty-five years is Martimmo Planno. His locks are awesome, his bearing regal. He has enormous authority over his people, and as a scholar. In 1961 he was one of the brethren who visited Ethiopia, and in 1966 during Haile Selassie's visit, he parted the seas of ecstatic worshippers so that the Emperor dared to leave his plane,escorting him to the King's House, Kingston, declaiming 'God has come!'

In his yard, study is central to the life of his followers, who serve a three-year appenticeship in the Bible, working right through the relevant parts. They then start all over again, for reinterpretation and debate are endless. In addition they learn Amharic and African history. One of his best-known pupils was Bob Marley, although they finally separated over matters of doctrine. 1978 was a particularly powerful year for him, because at the height of the city ghetto war, his revelation was of peace. 'Christmas' was celebrated on January 7. On January 8 a triple rainbow, symbol of peace, rose above Kingston and on January 9 a great call for peace went out throughout the land. Warring faction leaders responded, and it did seem that Rastafarian prophets might succeed where politicians had failed.

Brother God and Dread Heights

One solution to ghetto pressures is to follow the tradition of the early followers who settled out at Pinnacle, and go into the country. Here young followers, the 'youth', are removed from the violence, and their despair at disappointed expectations is lessened. In the city they are daily confronted by the lifestyle of the privileged. Recently Brother God, inspired by the Book of Isaiah, founded the Twelve Tribes of Israel in the hills at a camp called Dread Heights. As well as studying, the young are organized into football and cricket teams. These matches are an awesome sight — 'Dread flash him locks and weak heart drop!' But these activities, together with farming 'raising the things God taught us to name!' is secondary to the continuing motive for the community, 'to fulfil the people's wish to be repatriated to Ethiopia . . . Africa . . . not specifically Ethiopia.' It was to this group that Bob Marley affiliated after leaving Martimmo Planno.

Ras Sam Brown

Ras Sam Brown was born in Trelawney Parish in 1925. He is one of the most significant Rastafarians because of his qualities of prophet, thinker, poet and leader, and for the independent line he often takes. Some consider him a saint, others a bit of a rogue, but above all he is a realist who suffered with and for the poor with whom he lived at Back O'Wall before it was destroyed. It was this realism which made him stand as an Independent in the General Election of 1961, under the banner of the 'Black Man's Party'. He was not successful, but he was the first Rastafarian to try to engage in the national politics of Jamaica, instead of directing his energies towards other worldly goals.

In 1961 he set out the twenty-one points known as 'The Foundation of the Rastafarian Movement'. He believed that the movement should become more involved in politics. This made Rastafarianism more of a threat to conventional politicians. At the same time the young intellectuals, who before had held aloof from Rastafarianism because they were disenchanted with Jamaican politics and Christianity, were drawn towards cult membership. For the complete Charter, see the Appendix at the back of this book.

Despite the positive good Ras Sam Brown might have done in his campaign, he was rejected by the Rastafarians as a politial radical, but has gone on developing his philosophy, which is similar in its doctrines to the Black Power Movement in America.

A Rasta pedlar brings his woven bags to sell. To be financially independent is one of the believer's greatest wishes, and it is in these modest enterprises that he best succeeds

Prince Edward Emmanuel

While most groups remain very loosely organized, others tend to develop towards a more conventional church; Prince Edward Emmanuel has moved furthest in this direction, and away from the militancy of the Dreads. Most 'religious' of the cult leaders, the Prince worked within the Ethiopian National Congress, and his church is the Rastafarian Melchizedek Orthodox Church.

In particular this group has developed its reasoning on reincarnation. The Prince himself is felt by many of his followers to be the Black Christ; his cultists regard him with great reverence. They prostrate themselves during long periods of intense prayer.

The commune members divide their day between religion and providing themselves with a livelihood. They try to be self-sufficient, the Rastafarian ideal. They grow Ital food and make sandals.

In the meantime they wait for Repatriation, for as the Prince says, 'We only seek our daily food until the hour that the seven miles of ships of the Black Star Line come.'

5 The Rastafarians in Jamaica

The first Nyabingi
In 1958 the first convention of the various Rastafarian groups was held in Back O'Wall. It was intended that this convention (later called Nyabingi) should last a month. Exulting in their unity, and in expectation of early repatriation, on March 21 a group made a ritual 'capture' of the city by invading Victoria Park, waving their colours from prayer staffs held aloft. Later in the year they tried to capture the Old King's House in Spanish Town in the name of Haile Selassie. There were definite signs that the Rastafarians might try to establish Ethiopia-in-Exile while they awaited repatriation.

Publicity for the Rastafarians was mixed after the Nyabingi. There had been clashes with police concerning public order and in the months immediately afterwards they were severely harrassed for ganja possession. An effective way of humiliating them was to cut off their locks and shave their beards. There was ample evidence that the new confident mood of the Rastafarians might bring about more dramatic action, if something was not done about their grievances, but warnings to the authorities were ignored.

Reverend Claudius Henry
The Reverend Claudius Henry had been a visitor to the Nyabingi. He was a Jamaican resident in the United States, who had stayed on afterwards and started the African Reformed Church. On October 5 1959 hundreds of Rastafarians flocked to his church expecting immediate repatriation. The reason for this was that Henry had had printed hundreds of cards which sold at a shilling a time.

> Pioneering Israel's scattered children of African Origin "back home to Africa". This year 1959, deadline date - October 5th, this new government is God's Righteous Kingdom of Everlasting Peace on Earth. "Creation's Second Birth". Holder of this Certificate is requested to visit the Headquarters at 18 Rosalie Avenue, August 1st 1959 for our Emancipation Jubilee, commencing 9 a.m. sharp. Please reserve this Certificate for removal. No passport will be necessary for those returning to Africa, etc. We sincerely "The Seventh Emanuel's Brethren", gathering Israel's scattered and anointed prophet, Rev. C.V. Henry, R.B.

Given this 2nd day of March 1959 in the year of the reign of His Imperial Majesty, 1st Emperor of Ethiopia, God's Elect, Haile Selassie, King of Kings and Lord of Lords, Israel's returned Messiah.

Some people had even sold their houses and smallholdings in preparation for repatriation, and hundreds of people arrived at 18 Rosalie Avenue at the appointed time. Great hardship and humiliation was caused by this catastophe, and the 'false prophet' was sentenced to six years' goal, and his son took to the hills to train a Rastafarian group.

The 1960 Enquiry

The people had misread the language on the cards, but the Government did not, on this occasion, misread the desperation which their actions had demonstrated. This anxiety, the aftermath of the Nyabingi, shanty-town violence, the harrassment of the Rastafarians, were not ignored. Mr Samuel Lewis, Principal of the University College of the West Indies, set up an Enquiry, headed by H. G. Smith, R. Augier and Rex Nettleford to enquire into the Rastafarian faith and the discontent of its members. This Enquiry made ten main recommendations and the Hon. Norman Manley, Premier of Jamaica, felt it was most important for these recommendations to be put into practice.

The recommendations of the 1960 Enquiry
1 The Government of Jamaica should send a mission to African countries to arrange for immigration of Jamaicans. Representatives of the Ras Tafari brethren should be included in the mission.
2 Preparations should be discussed immediately with representatives of the Ras Tafari brethren.
3 The general public should realize that the great majority of Ras Tafari brethren are peaceful citizens, willing to do an honest day's work.
4 The police should complete their security enquiries rapidly and cease to persecute peaceful Ras Tafari brethren.
5 The building of low-rent housing should be accelerated, and provision made for self-help and cooperative building.
6 Government should acquire the principal areas where squatting is now taking place, and arrange for water, light, sewage disposal and collection of rubbish.
7 Civic centres should be built with facilities for technical classes,

youth clubs, child clinics etc. The churches and the University College of the West Indies should cooperate.

8 The Ethiopian Orthodox Coptic Church should be invited to establish a branch in the West Indies.

9 Ras Tafari brethren should be assisted to establish cooperative workshops.

10 Press and radio facilities should be accorded to leading members of the movement.

Most of these recommendations were fulfilled more or less successfully, the last being the establishment of the Ethiopian Orthodox Church in 1969. What the Enquiry did do was to acknowledge that, for the time being, Rastafarians were living in intolerable conditions in Jamaica. Although Rastafarian unity lay in their religion, their day to day living conditions could be improved. The idea of 'rehabilitating Babylon' grew up alongside that of immediate repatriation.

The respect and seriousness with which the Report treated the Rastafarians enabled other Jamaicans to regard them seriously. A growing number of middle-class sympathizers and university students began to associate with the Rastafarians.

Jamaican Independence
For all Rastafarians the Jamaican Independence in 1962 seemed paradoxical. Many smallholders who had sold their land for bauxite mining and who had stayed in Jamaica, felt doubly disinherited. The alternatives to traditional occupations, then as now, were to work for an international corporation, probably American, or in the tourist trade. To the Rastafarian, this would be humiliating work which would seem too much like house-slavery in the old days.

The motto of Jamaica may be 'Out of Many, One People', but for the Rastafarian this contradicts his need to create a feeling of black nationhood, which emphasizes his shared identity with the other scattered black people throughout the world.

Back O'Wall
Back O'Wall was one of the most depressing shanty-town areas of Kingston. The violence and general unease in the area increased after Independence, largely because the expectations of a better life had been disappointed. Sam Brown and other brethren lived there, and it was easy to focus blame for vandalism and gang warfare on the Rastafarians.

Leonard Barrett was an eyewitness on July 12 1965, when two hundred and fifty police armed with guns, bayonets, pistols and clubs

Although Back O'Wall has disappeared, living conditions for the poorer urban dweller are not easy. While the poorest squat at the outskirts of cities, many others live in very congested and difficult conditions

assembled. The shanty dwellers, in the flimsiest of shacks, had no warning till they saw bulldozers thundering down the road towards them. Most of them were too stunned to do anything except scramble out of the bulldozers' path and watch the destruction of their homes. A few tried to salvage their scant possessions. Just as if the world had ended, a great fire consumed the remnants of the first encampment, while the fire tenders stood by and did nothing. Barrett reports:

> The sorrows and sufferings of the people were too much to report. In three days, three camps were destroyed and hundreds of people were left abandoned with only the rags on their backs. Hundreds simply moved into the nearby graveyard, setting up temporary shelters; others found some comfort at the Spanish Town Roman Catholic Church and others simply lodged on sidewalks.

The Rastafarian Movement Recruitment Centre of Ras Sam Brown and the African National Congress of Prince Edward Emmanuel were destroyed. Many people blamed the Rastafarians for their hardship but others, as well as Rastafarians, saw the event in prophetic terms — yet one more scourging of the people by the oppressors. The significant difference was that these were the political oppressors of an 'Independent' Jamaica. The Rastafarians' desire for repatriation was rekindled, and although one intention in destroying Back O'Wall had been to control their influence, the fact that they were forced into other areas of the city both spread their message, and enabled others to see them and them to see themselves as martyrs.

The visit of Haile Selassie
On April 25 1966 came the visit of the Emperor Haile Selassie. For four amazing days the Rastafarians celebrating his coming. Initially the announcement was seen as a token of immediate repatriation and frenzied preparation had been made.

On the day of his arrival, a vast crowd assembled at the airport, about 10,000 of whom were Rastafarians. It was raining very hard; the brethren said that as soon as their God came, it would stop — and, miraculously, it did. Martimmo Planno cleared a path for the Emperor through the surging crowds — having just had to persuade him to leave the plane. Haile Selassie was obviously moved by his overwhelming welcome, and wept as he saw the people, and their flags, and heard the commotion.

Although no one asked Haile Selassie if he were God, the

Emperor spoke through his interpreter and said, 'Holy Priests and Warriors are The Dreadlock Rastafarians, and I am He.'

The medals and cards distributed in commemoration of the day are still treasured, and the day itself is celebrated as the greatest Rastafarian Holy Day. In a sense Ethiopia had come to Jamaica, so, although repatriation appeared even more imminent, the brethren felt a great desire, given the confidence and recognition which the visit had given them, to liberate themselves *before* the great departure.

Michael Manley, Moses, or . . .

Michael Manley, Prime Minister of Jamaica, until he was defeated by Edward Seaga in the General Election in 1980, used Rastafarian symbols and reference to draw cult loyalty. he is the son of Norman Manley, first Prime Minister of Independent Jamaica, who did so

The climax of the Peace Concert, April 1978, with the then Prime Minister Manley and the leader of the opposition, Edward Seaga, raising hands with Bob Marley.

Rastamen and whites discuss conditions in the ghetto. On the right, Claudie Massop and Bucky Marshall, formerly notorious gangsters, have now made peace and embraced the Rasta message of goodwill

much to implement the findings of the 1960 Enquiry. He identifies himself with Joshua, son of Moses, and the reincarnative associations operated powerfully for the Prime Minister.

In 1972 his People's Party cultivated youth groups — and those with Rastafarian associations in particular, together with their reggae cult heroes. Manley himself visited Ethiopia and came back with a staff given him by Haile Selassie, which he called his 'Rod of Correction'. Thousands of Jamaicans, not just Rastafarians, began to believe that the Rod had supernatural powers. Many Rastafarians were uneasy, but prepared to come to terms if social advantages were to be gained. More Rastafarians warmed to him when he freed first-time ganja offenders from prison.

Since then conditions in Jamaica, and particularly in Kingston, have worsened with gang warfare reaching horrific proportions. Rastafarians who had supported Manley were disenchanted. The living standards of the poor had not improved. The 1976 election was very unsatisfactory. Bob Marley, most famous of the cult figures, who had appeared on stage with Manley, left the island after having escaped from a machine-gun attack. Conditions in Trenchtown,

Kingston, were so violent that the cinema erected a concrete screen to deflect bullets. Gun Courts were set up to handle the escalating gun crimes and violence. The Rastafarians felt that they had delivered their part in the political pact and received nothing in return.

After a long period of withdrawal from the world, directing their energies to the actual repatriation, most Rastafarians now feel it is necessary to look to improving this world, to rehabilitation. Their religious language is revolutionary in tone, and one development in their faith would be to translate their sacred language into revolution. Graffitti say 'Unite for Revolution, not gang war' which is the opposite of the Rasta creed of 'Peace and Love'. However what the Rastafarians see as Manley's betrayal strengthens their belief that it is the Rastafarians, not the politicians, who understand the people and therefore hold the real power. 'They (the politicians) look upon us as obeah men, but we control the hearts and minds of men all over the world,' warns Blackheart. There seems every indication that he may be right.

In the autumn of 1980 there was a General Election in Jamaica. In a landslide victory Edward Seaga defeated Michael Manley.

It is too soon to summarize what effect his policies will have on Jamaica generally but his appointment will inevitably result in a change in direction.

6   The Rastafarians in Britain

Parents and children

Most Caribbean immigrants came to Britain in the 1950s. Government policy was to encourage West Indians to settle in the large cities and work in low status jobs. However, menial jobs in Britain were better than unemployment at home, and at least the immigrants could dream of the chances of their children — the next generation.

Most of this generation of parents started, or joined, Pentecostal Churches. The churches helped them keep in touch with the gossip and news back home, as very often the members came from similar areas in the same islands. They also helped the immigrants to come to terms with and make sense of their disappointing and dispiriting situation in Britain.

Nearly all of this generation — now the generation of parents — wanted to become part of the British way of life. Their children — British-born blacks or recent immigrants — are very different. They are aware of their own abilities and do not see why they should do poorly paid, low status work. Sadly, this realization comes at a time when unemployment makes it unlikely that they will be able to get *any* work. They refuse just to accept the situation. A young black sums up his feelings in *Talking Blues:*

> I and I really want to go home. But as I say, we don't even have
> no dunsi fi buy some food out a the road, before we go say go
> home. And we know say dem white man ya have it fi give I and
> I, and we entitled to it. I man no know wa a go on, you know.
> But is that I man would like to find out, wa a go on? And I man a call 'pon
> the leader dem fi come forward and show us what a go on, because
> things bad, man. We condition what we a live in a worse than a dog.
> Education bad. Right now the youth dem I man can talk but there is
> always somebody else, there is all the youth dem wa fi come. Dem
> don't have nothing. We don't have nothing. So what we a go show
> dem when dem come? Nothing. So right now I many would a like
> these so-called black youth leaders and dem community people and
> Social Security and all dem people dey fi forward dem self and
> show I and I wa dem a go on with. Well anyway, if dem no do it,
> we a go forward. And that mean to say is either blood a go run,
> or fire a go burn, or water a go drown.

Unlike their parents, young people are aware and proud of their colour. They are more likely to reject a world which will not accept them on their own terms. Linton Kwesi Johnson, although he is not a Rastafarian himself, describes the situation in *Yout Rebel*:

a bran new breed of blacks
have now emerged . . .
they can only be
new in age
but not in rage,
not needin'
the soft and also
shallow councillin
of the soot-brained
sage in chain;
carvin a new path
moving forward to freedom.

In Britain, as in Jamaica, Rastafarianism provides a powerful answer for many of these young blacks, their response to unemployment, grinding urban depression and social 'downpression'.

The 1960s and 1970s
In Britain there were few Rastafarian sympathizers in 1960. Their attempt, with others, to express their black national identity in the British Black Power Movement was disillusioning, so it was partly as a result of this disappointment that Immanuel Fox, Gabriel Adams and others founded the Universal Black Improvement Society. Its aim was to develop black consciousness, and the seeds of British Rastafarianism were planted.

In London in 1968 a branch of the Ethiopian World Federation was founded, together with a branch of the Ethiopian Orthodox Church. It was through the EWF that the first group of Rastafarians came together.

Knowledge of the faith came from several sources. There were a few brethren from Jamaica who had migrated. There was the oral tradition of Garveyism, together with his books. There were the popular music and lyrics coming out of the Caribbean, together with accounts from those who went home on visits, and the black press.

Almost immediately after the first branch was formed, a group broke away forming itself into a British branch of the Jamaican 'Twelve Tribes of Israel' of Brother God. As well as various groups, there were the individual prophets who operated singly or within very small and informal groupings. The groups provided opportunities for reasoning and debate, based on Biblical interpretation, and a warm brotherhood of friendship and mutual support. Each group built up its own oral tradition of the faith. The members were mostly young and from Pentecostal or Roman Catholic families.

Residence and survival

The early 1970s saw the beginnings of squatting. The conflict between parents and children about staying out at night and getting up in the morning led to many young blacks being thrown out of home. Squatting was a way of finding somewhere to live if you had no money and no job. Rundown empty property awaiting renovation or demolition was colonized by groups of young Rastafarians, the most significant instances of this being in Handsworth, Birmingham. Despite their decay, they provided shelter in the urban jungle, and their use has developed.

Feelings of brotherhood and cooperation are easily developed in such a situation, as is the self-sufficient and ascetic life of the Rastafarian. In some communes a high-developed and disciplined lifestyle emerged, with religious study central to life, as it had been in the Pinnacle days. Locks were grown, tams and high caps worn, and emblems and slogans decorated the squats. Members' clothes reflected their poverty, but even this was turned to advantage. What had been the too-short trousers and the overlong overcoats of the impoverished, were worn with style and confidence. Considerable ingenuity was used to embellish clothes with the Rastafarian colours.

Reggae

Reggae has always been inseparable from Rastafarianism. Despite its wide acceptance by whites, the 'secrecy' of reggae is maintained. In Britain, Rastafarian brotherhoods enjoy the music and explore the symbolism of the lyrics, which whites continue to misinterpret. Linton Kwesi Johnson, in his book *Bass Culture,* describes what reggae is to Rastafarians:

> musik of blood
> black reared
> pain rooted
> heart-geared.

The affiliation of the groups is made clear — the members of Steel Pulse comment at the end of the sleeve notes of *Tribute to the Martyrs:*

Ronnie	It can never be wong to believe Truth & right
David	Jah dis Jah dat
Phonso	No isim a gydim
Steve	As it was it shall be
Basil	Soon come.

The beliefs and symbols of Rastafarians in Britain are very similar to those in Jamaica because British members look to the traditional sources of Rastafarian inspiration. One of the finest British reggae examples of this is *Tribute to the Martyrs* by Steel Pulse:

It was a hard task
To take on
To make us all believe
To rescue us from evil cause
They wanted to achieve
Avenge to gain respect
Defend ourselves to the end

A Rasta band in Kingston. Although groups do use sound systems, young Rastas are quick to improvise instruments

47

Patriots of dark continent
I give all of my confidence
Redemption . . .

Weh dem gone
Weh dem deh

Tribute to the martyrs
Which part them gone
A weh dem deh, Heh

When Martyrs died they save our lives
They had an early grave
Sacrifice has taken place
For the chosen race heh

Which part dem gone
Which part deh . . .

There was one they crucified
Dead men tell no tales
There were some they hung so high
We know the reason why
Caught, and tried, bound and beat
Locked, locked away inside
But won their war of words
Patriots lost their lives
Yet no-one cries
The whole world stands accused.

Which part dem gone
Which part of dem deh . . .
A multitude of people
Dem try dem best to convince
Only to capture the heart of a few
The truth you can't dismiss
They are telling me silent waters run deep.
So their knowledge I'll always seek.
They are telling me
A nation without its past history
Is like a tree without roots.

Which part dem gone
Which part dem deh . . .

Best to strike when irons hot,
It will not bend when cold . . .

Not too late to learn my friend
Wisdom ripes with old age, if you got it
Now wake up you distressed, yeh yeh yeh
Under, under oppressed man afflication
Hell fire can't be quenched with water, no sah!
Though it once had a dreadful shower of rain
We who are blessed they just can't put us under
Martyrs golden text is bondage never again
If not by free will it then by force
Break the bondgage plot that course.

Remember . . .
Message preach to all, you hear something

Doctrine for the soul, you feel something
The story has been told, you know something
Now answer, martyrs call, do something
Prophesize the fall
Backs against the wall no more, be something.

Which part dem gone
Which part dem gone.

Popular Rastafarian bands retain their social commitment. Here, *The
Meditations* **play with other groups at a concert for 25,000 fans to raise
funds for the deprived areas of Kingston. The popularity of Jamaican
groups in the UK is great; many excellent British black groups continue to
develop the musical tradition**

Another outstanding example from the same source is the following dialogue:

Gooseneck	Homage to the Martyrs[1]
Inity	Tribute to the Martyrs
Gooseneck	Love it, it suit a man
	to set example like
	Toussaint L'Ouverture chase all
	oppressor man out of his land.
	Quick.
Size 9	Hey stepper is what
	happen to Bogle?
Stepper	Morant Bay rebellion
	standing up feh 'im rights
	dem decide fe hang 'im up.
Size 9	WHAT?
Stepper	Truly.
Gooseneck	1865
Stepper	So Greyseed what you hear 'bout Jackson
Greyseed	George Jackson.
	imprisonment
	- solitary confinement.
Inity	Pow! Pow! Aaaaaahhhhhh!
Gooseneck	1971
Greyseed	Bumbo . . .
Bumbo	Yes Greyseed?
Greyseed	WHAT happen to Marcus?
Bumbo	Marcus say a thing sah.
Inity	ONE GOD, ONE AIM, ONE DESTINY
Gooseneck	Starliner
Inity	Black
Size 9	Hey is wha happen to Biko

[1] This song refers to the following people, regarded by Rastas as martyrs to the cause of all Black people:

Toussaint l'Ouverture: Haitian hero and national leader

Paul Bogle: Jamaican Baptist deacon and preacher, associated with the 1865 Morant Bay Rebellion

George Jackson: American Black Panther, shot and killed in 1971 while allegedly trying to escape from San Quentin prison; one of the 'Soledad Brothers'

Martin Luther King: Civil rights campaigner and Churchman, a national American hero, assassination on 4 April 1968

Malcolm X: Murdered in 1965, under the name of Al Hadj Malik al-Shabazz, which he took after a pilgrimage to Mecca. Originally a Black Muslim, he formed the Organization of Afro-American Unity.

Steve Biko: South African student leader, campaigner for the rights of Blacks, murdered in 1977.

50

Gooseneck	Biko detainee
	in detention - Vank
Size 9	What?
Gooseneck	1977
Size 9	South Africa
Bumbo	The Black Panthers
Inity	Freedom Fighters!
Gooseneck	They tried them died.
Grizzly	Luther King
Gooseneck	He had a dream grizzly
	He had a dream
	believe you me
Bumbo	Malcolm X
Inity	LIFT STRUGGLE
Gooseneck	In pool of blood 1965
Stepper	But wait —
	nobody don't leave?
Gooseneck	Is only we Rasta
Inity	Yes I
Gooseneck	I and I was not born
	rich nor poor.
	I and I was born naked.
Inity	You hear something
	feel something
	know something
	do something
	see something
	BE SOMEONE
	. . . (fade)

Bob Marley and the Wailers

At the time the squats were being established, the impact of reggae was first fully felt in the United Kingdom with the tour by the Wailers to promote *Catch a Fire* with its intense 'Slave Driver' track.

Slave driver a table is turn,
Catch a fire so you can get burn
Slave driver the table is turn
Catch a fire you gonna get burn.
Everytime I hear a crack of the whip
My blood runs cold
I remember in the Slave ship
How they brutalize my very soul.

The tour was immensely successful and significant. It was aimed at student audiences in the universities, and it acted in rather the same way as the 1960 University Enquiry Report in the West Indies. It brought the movement to the notice of privileged intellectuals as well as the Mods, Rude Boys and Rastafarians. Soon afterwards another tour promoted *Burnin'* with the 'Get Up, Stand Up' track which was interpreted as encouraging brethren to recognize their Rastafarian inner consciousness — and act! And in 1974 came the *Natty Dread* album. Marley was already a British cult figure, but his lyrical and religious fervour, together with his appearance, made him *the* cult figure for the Rastafarians. In Marley, many saw a recincarnation of Marcus Garvey, the great prophet. This conviction stimulated a great response, particularly in London, where Rastafarians became more 'visible'. Bob Marley became the same sort of hero that Garvey had been for an earlier generation. Tragically, he died of cancer aged thirty-six, on 11 May 1981.

Left: Bob Marley

Above: His Eminence Abouna Yesehaq, Archbishop of the Ethiopian Orthodox Church spreads incense over the coffin of Bob Marley, while Rita Marley, his widow, mourns. After the service, Bob Marley's body was accompanied by thousands of mourners to a hillside tomb. The publicity of his funeral contrasts markedly with the remote place where he now lies, which is much closer to the peaceful centre of Rastafarian beliefs

A great world audience, as well as Rastafarians in Jamaica and the UK, mourned Bob Marley's tragic death at the age of thirty-six on 11 May 1981. The funeral was a great national event and took place in the Ethiopian Orthodox Church

The Death of Haile Selassie

As in Jamaica, the British Rastafarians adjusted to the news of the death of Haile Selassie on August 27 1975. It had taken place in revolutionary and mysterious circumstances, so the information about his death was vague, but what was inescapable was the picture given by press and television of Haile Selassie as an oppressive and cruel tyrant.

The Rastafarians were concerned not with explanations of Ras Tafari's behaviour but of his death. Some said that he was still alive; others said that he had atomized and materialized in another form and age; others said that he could choose to reveal himself in whichever form that he chose — and Haile Selassie had been his latest, greatest manifestation. Most agreed that the white world had furthered its conspiracy against the black by his removal, and that by ignoring this trick, the white man's machinations would be defeated.

Ernest Cashmore calls this the 'Babylonian Conspiracy' and explains how Rastafarians have interpreted the situation:

1   The Rastas are the reincarnation of the ancient tribes of Israel who had been enslaved and kept in exile by their white oppressors, the agents of Babylon.
2   The entire history of the black man since his contact with whites, should be understood in terms of systematic denial of freedom — every event in colonization was a recycle of the same pattern.
3   This was an attempt to suppress the black man.
4   Haile Selassie is the true God. Some blacks were snared into Christianity, but the Rastafarians saw through the conspiracy.
5   Haile Selassie is not truly dead.

Having adjusted their doctrines in this way, some Rastafarians felt that they could be baptized in the Ethiopian Orthodox Church in London. The Abba (Bishop) had agreed to conduct the services, on the understanding that their locks were cut off and that they renounced the 'heresy' of the divinity of Haile Selassie. Some members could not compromise and turned their backs on the Church. In 1976, however, some brethren were baptized. In general, Rastafarian membership of the Church has not increased greatly. The truly dramatic growth, since 1974, and particularly since 1976, has been in the individual personal recognition of 'Rasta identity'.

'Downpression'

Whereas in the first years Dreadlocks had been seen as harmless 'weirdos', by the second half of the seventies the vast growth in the movement among the black population had led to a variety of threatened responses from the media, the authorities, and the police in particular. A vicious circle of associations built up based on the mad bad black Rastafarian theme. Much of this fear was built on the great misconceptions, such as the 1976 *Reading Mail* report of the Rastafarians as a 'black Mafia'. In 1977 a report was commissioned on the Handsworth situation, which examined the Rastafarian tension with the police. It isolated the Rastafarians as the 'problem'. It focussed on non conformist behaviour instead of on suggesting ways of using wasted talent in self-help and cooperative ventures. The religious significance of the movement, with its dual insistence on Haile Selassie's divinity and the need for repatriation from Babylon, was nearly ignored.

In 1978 *The Observer* reported that 'Rastafarianism has taken hold, either as a religion, or as a style of black consciousness, on the imaginations of Jamaican youths in the UK . . . It is the most powerful cultural force among Jamaicans and black youths in Britain.'

To be a Rastafarian poses problems. Despite their creed of 'Peace and Love' Rastafarians often have trouble with the police because of breaking the drug laws. Black sympathizers in the community see the problem, for however strong the faith, to act out a life based on peace and love in a violent urban situation may be too difficult.

There is the Rasta group. They dictate peace and love but they are confronted by their need to survive in the community alongside with the need to be committed to peace and love.

Talking Blues

The harassment from the police and the majority culture has been very real:

Yes, the violence of the oppressor runnin' wild;
them picking up the yout them fe suss;
Powell prophesying a black, a black, a black conquest;
and the National Front is on the rampage
making fire bombs fe burn we.

O that history should take such a rough route,
causing us this bitterness and pain on the way,
is a room full of a fact you can't walk out . . .

Doun de Road Linton Kwesi Johnson

One consolation for the Rastafarian is his sense of identity and association with martyrs of the past, and the freedom that he discovers in his self-awareness, and the Rastafarian dignity which helps him rise above harassment.

Babylon was life in Jamaica, and Britain has proved to be an even more punishing experience for many Rastafarians. Rastafarianism is black and black is Africa. Britain is Babylon. White is Babylon. The police are Babylon. A young Rastafarian sums up with this fairly typical assertion:

We want to go home. We don't want to stay here no more. We want a grant to set up ourselves when we go over there. We don't want to depend on our own people over there. We want dem to give us what we need and let us go over there. We want to be free. We want to go to our father's land where you brought us from. Oh Lord! Save I and I that are in this hell. We want to go where the sun is shining where I can be free in my forefathers' land. I know I am a slave. I can't take it no longer.

Free I. Free I.
I don't want to steal. I can't get no job. Your job you offer I is
what you offer dogs. The law treat us like animals.

I have been to jail. I know what it is like. It is disgrace. They try
to brainwash us. But it is only my faith, oh Father. It is only my
faith. I know their system (and) how it works. You can't fool I
no more. Your days are numbered. I don't want no favours. I
just want to be free like a bird in the tree.

Today

The central beliefs of Rastafarians have survived since their formu-
lation. They have proved that they are capable of adaptation and
reinterpretation when necessary, and there seems no reason, in the
1980s, to believe that the faith will not continue to grow steadily in
membership, although it seems likely that the membership will remain
young.

The symbols of Rastafarianism are powerful and widely recognized,
and treated with respect, or distrust, if not reverence and tolerance by
the outsider. They indicate not only a member's religious beliefs, but
also his demand, as a part of his faith, to be seen and acknowledged in
his blackness.

In Britain, where the Rastafarians are purely urban groups, self-
sufficiency is made even harder when subsistence farming and fishing
are not available. It is probable that family lifestyles will differ in
Britain for the rising generations of children born in Britain to
Rastafarians. Those in Jamaica will continue to depend on their
mothers for food, clothing and general care, whereas in Britain more
father-orientated families will probably emerge. It may be that un-
married Rastafarian women will play a more significant, more
assertive role in the UK; in Jamaica they are insignificant in a religious
sense.

A comment from a member of Steel Pulse sums up the situation:
'All you've got to turn to is your own culture and yourself.'

Appendix

Charter of the Rastafarians

1   Members of the Rastafarian Movement are an inseparable part of the Black people of Jamaica (Every African a Rasta!)

2   As such we cannot and do not proclaim any higher aims than the legitimate aims and aspirations of the Black people of Jamaica.

3   The Rastafarian Movement consists of the most advanced, determined and uncompromising fighters against discrimination, ostracism and oppression of the Black people of Jamaica.

4   The Rastafarian Movement stands for freedom in its fullest sense and for the recovery, dignity, self-respect and sovereignty of the Black people of Jamaica.

5   Many deplore and accuse the Black people of raising the colour question in this island. But White Supremacy was the official policy of this island for hundreds of years and white supremacists never regarded black men as the dogs in their yards.

6   To white supremacy has been added Brown men supremacy and the mongrel children of the Black women came to think and behave contemptuously of Black people.

7   Time has removed some of the grosser aspects of White/Brown man supremacy; but discrimination, disrespect and abuse of Black people are still here in many forms.

8   For instance, in their employment policies, the big guns get generous salaries, house allowance, travelling expenses and bonuses. The poor Black man working in the same industry or enterprise cannot get adequate food, money and has to accept poor treatment and insults as part of the price of holding the job.

9   In their housing policy, they have houses for the rich, housing for the middle class and housing for the under-privileged. 'Underprivileged' is only another name in Jamaica for poor Black people.

10   God did not say 'come let us make underprivileged man, middle-class man and rich man'. He said 'Come let us make man'. The existence of underprivileged man in Jamaica is a product of White and Brown men supremacy.

11   The Rastafarian Movement has as its chief aim the complete destruction of all vestiges of white suprem-acy in Jamaica, thereby putting an end to economic exploitation and the social degradation of the Black people.

12   **The Rastafarian Movement stands for Repatriation and power and for the fullest cooperation and inter-course between the Governments and people of Africa and a free and independent people of Jamaica.**

13   The Rastafarian Movement, for the furtherance of these ends, must have the backing of its support to, or lead, a political movement of its own.

14   The Rastafarian Movement has the backing of no party. We are subject to persecution and discrimina-tion.

15   The Rastafarian Movement has lent its support to the two big parties, this support has been in vain because no improvement has taken place in our condition. Neither are we offered, nor do we see, any hope.

16   The Rastafarian Movement has therefore decided to actively join the political struggle and create a political Movement with the aim of *taking power* and implement measures for the uplift of the poor and oppressed.

17   Because we have no other aims but the legitimate aims of all Black people on this island, this movement is open to all Black people, irrespective of class, religion or financial standing.

18   We are not declaring against the political leadership of White men or Brown men because of their colour,

but because of the wickedness that they represent, and invite them to repent.

19   Consequently, if a man is as Black as night, his colour is in our estimation of no avail if he is an oppressor and destroyer of his people.

20   All men therefore are free irrespective of colour to join this political crusade. The only condition is that they must abandon evil.

21   Suffering Black people of Jamaica, let us unite and set up a righteous Government under the slogan of *Repatriation and Power.*

List of further reading

Non-fiction

Barrett, L. (1977) *Rastafarians: The Dreadlocks of Jamaica* Heinemann

Brown, R. (due 1982) *The Complete Rastafari Bible* Bogle l'Ouverture

Bishton, D. and Homer, B. (1978) *Talking Blues* AFFOR, 1 Finch Road, Lozells, Birmingham. This booklet has accounts from Rastafarians who live in Birmingham today.

Cashmore, E. (1979) *Rastaman: The Rastafarian Movement in England* George Allen & Unwin

Garrison, L. (1979) *Black Youth, Rastafarianism: the Identity Crisis* ACER

Nichols, T. and Sparrow, B. (1979) *Rastafari: A Way of Life* Anchor Books

Owens, J. (1980) *Dread: the Rastafaria of Jamaica* Heinemann

Plummer, J. (1980) *The Movement of the Jah People* Press Gang

Fiction

Mais, R. (1974) *Brother Man* Heineman

Paterson, O. (1974) *Children of Sisyphus* Bolivar Press

Poetry

Johnson, L.K. (1975) *Dread, Beat and Blood* Bogle l'Ouverture. This is a book of vivid verse, by a non-Rastafarian, which nevertheless conveys much of the feel of the British black scene within which Rastafarianism is developing.

Index

Index by Ann Edwards

Also from Ward Lock Educational:

The Arts and Practices of Living Religions
Series Editor: John R. Hinnells

This series introduces readers to different religions as they are
practised in daily life and expressed through the arts. It studies how
people convey their religious experience through dress, dance, drama,
music, writing, painting, sculpture, the places where they worship and
the objects used in their ceremonies. It is concerned as much with
simple, homely art forms as with splendid works of art; with emotions
as well as beliefs. Each book will provide readers with a stimulating,
fresh insight into the living spirit of the many facets of each religion
and add an extra dimension to its study.

Judaism *Alan Unterman*
0 7062 4126 6

Christianity *Peter Moore*
0 7062 4125 8

Islam *Joan Allgrove*
0 7062 4127 4

Buddhism *Peter Harvey*
0 7062 4128 2